ROCKS, MINERALS AND RESOURCES

P9-CSE-971

Metals

John Zronik

Crabtree Publishing Company

www.crabtreebooks.com

Crabtree Publishing Company

www.crabtreebooks.com

Coordinating editor: Ellen Rodger

Editors: Sean Charlebois, Carrie Gleason

Production coordinator: Rosie Gowsell

Design: Samara Parent

Proofreader and Indexer: Adrianna Morganelli

Art director: Rob MacGregor

Photo research: Allison Napier

Consultant: Dr. Richard Cheel, Professor of Earth Sciences, Brock University

Photographs: © James L. Amos/CORBIS/MAGMA: p. 15 (bottom); © Bettmann/CORBIS/MAGMA: p. 11 (bottom right), p. 13; © Martin Bond/Photo Researchers, Inc.: p. 26; © Peter Bowater/Photo Researchers, Inc.: p. 23; © Peter/Georgina Bowater/Mira.com: p. 20; © CORBIS/MAGMA: p. 21 (bottom right); © Eye of Science/Photo Researchers, Inc.: p. 24; © Richard Frear/Photo Researchers, Inc.: p. 7 (bottom left); © Robert Garvey/CORBIS/MAGMA: p. 28; Carrie Gleason: p. 30 (bottom left); © Pascal Goetgheluck/Photo Researchers, Inc.: p. 14 (bottom right); Pascal Goetgheluck/Science Photo Library: p. 17 (top right); Margot Granitsa/The Image Works: p. 22; © Klaus Guldbrandsen/ Photo Researchers, Inc.: p. 17 (bottom right); © Lindsay Hebberd/ CORBIS/MAGMA: p. 6 (top right); Hulton Archive/Getty Images: p. 12 (top right); © Archivo Iconografico, S.A./CORBIS/MAGMA: p. 10; The Image Bank/Getty Images: p. 21 (top left); © Andrew Lambert Photography/Photo Researchers, Inc.: p. 14 (top right); Erich Lessing/Art Resources, NY: p. 11 (top left), p. 12 (bottom left); © Christophe Loviny/CORBIS /MAGMA: p. 9 (top); © John Madere/CORBIS/MAGMA: p. 6 (bottom); Michael J. O'Brien: p. 29 (top right); Samara Parent: p. 25 (bottom left); © Charles Philip /CORBIS /MAGMA: p. 29 (bottom); © Chris R. Sharp/ Photo Researchers, Inc.: p. 18; Stone/Getty Images: p. 30 (top right); © U.S. Department of Energy/Photo Researchers, Inc.: p. 19 (top right); © Charles D. Winters/Photo Researchers, Inc.: p. 7 (top right), p. 16 (both), p. 17 (middle left); © Tim Wright/CORBIS/ MAGMA: p. 19 (bottom)

Illustrations: Jim Chimpyshenko: p. 15 (top); Roman Goforth: pg. 3; Dan Pressman: p. 8, p. 9 (bottom), p. 27; David Wysotski: pp. 4-5

Cover: The ancient Chimu people of South America made beautiful funeral masks out of precious metals such as gold.

Title page: Steel beams used to make buildings stronger crisscross each other on a modern construction site.

Back cover: Old cars are sold for scrap metal and then pounded down and reused to make other metal products.

Crabtree Publishing Company

www.crabtreebooks.com   1-800-387-7650

Cataloging-in-Publication Data

Zronik, John Paul.
    Metals / written by John Paul Zronik.
        p. cm. -- (Rocks, minerals, and resources)
    Includes index.
    ISBN 0-7787-1418-7 (rlb) -- ISBN 0-7787-1450-0 (pbk)
    1. Metals--Juvenile literature. 2. Mines and mineral resources--Juvenile
literature. I. Title. II. Series.
    TN148.Z76 2005
    669--dc22
                                            2004012808
                                            LC

Published in the United States
PMB 16A
350 Fifth Ave.
Suite 3308
New York, NY
10118

Published in Canada
616 Welland Ave.
St. Catharines
Ontario, Canada
L2M 5V6

Published in the United Kingdom
73 Lime Walk
Headington
Oxford
OX3 7AD
United Kingdom

Published in Australia
386 Mt. Alexander Rd.
Ascot Vale (Melbourne)
V1C 3032

Contents

Earth metal in space

The twin rocket
boosters roar as the
space shuttle rises upward
from the launch pad. Carrying
seven crew members, the shuttle will
travel through Earth's atmosphere in less than nine
minutes. In space, it will orbit the Earth at speeds of up to 17,500
miles per hour (28,163 km/h) on its eleven-day mission. Venturing
into space is made possible, in part, because of the materials used
to construct the shuttle. The specialized metals
used in the space shuttle, such as aluminum, can
withstand intense pressure and heat during the
space flight.

The value of metal

From building the space shuttle to preserving food in tin cans, people depend on metals every day of their lives. Almost everything we make or use today contains some amount of metal. Even if an object is not made of metal, there is a good chance it was built using tools made of metal. Humans have been using metals for more than 5,000 years. Tools and weapons were the first objects made from metals.

What are metals?

Metals are minerals, or substances that form naturally below the surface of the Earth. Metals are inorganic, which means they are made of substances that were never alive. Metals are found in mineral-rich rock called ore. Ore is a mixture of rock, metal, and small amounts of other elements.

Metal properties

Most metals are lustrous, or shiny. People have sought lustrous metals such as gold and silver for thousands of years, giving them high **economic** value. Metals are also good **conductors** of heat and **electricity**. This means metals can be used to transfer heat and electricity from one place to another. Some metals, such as copper, conduct heat and electricity better than others. Most metals are strong and durable, meaning they do not **deteriorate** easily. Iron is a very hard and durable metal. Others, such as lead, are softer and less durable. Metals are also ductile, which means they can easily be reshaped into a different form.

(above) One of the earliest known uses of the metals gold and silver was as jewelry.

(right) Most metals are buried deep under the Earth's surface. The copper at this mine is extracted in levels, called open-pit mining.

Alloys

A metal made by combining different types of metals is called an alloy. Alloys are made to increase a metal's strength, to make it more **resistant** to **corrosion** and wear, to make it lighter, and even to change its color. To make alloys, a metal is melted down and combined with other metals. Copper is a metal used in many alloys because it is **abundant**, lustrous, and easy to shape. Brass is an alloy which is made by combining copper with zinc.

(below) Bronze is used to make bells that ring out from churches and government buildings around the world. Bronze is also used to make sculptures and statues.

Ferrous metals

Ferrous metals are metals that contain iron. They are the most commonly used metals today. Iron is a heavy, silver-white metal and is one of the most abundant metals in the Earth's crust. Steel is a ferrous metal, made by mixing iron, carbon, and small amounts of other elements. Ferrous metals are used in construction and industry, including making metal bridges and high-rise buildings. Metals that do not contain iron are known as non-ferrous metals.

(above) The metal copper is used to make electrical wire because it is a good conductor of electricity.

Ore deposits

Metal minerals form in magma. Magma is hot, melted rock that lies deep under the Earth's crust, or its hard, rocky outer layer. Metal minerals reach the surface of the Earth when the magma rises during a volcanic eruption.

From the depths

Volcanoes are vents in the crust through which magma and steam escape from the depths of the Earth. When a volcano erupts, magma flows from it as lava. Lava cools and hardens into rock. Almost all rocks contain metal minerals. Ore deposits form in places where magma that flows from a volcano contains a high amount of metal minerals. When mineral-rich magma cools, it hardens into ore.

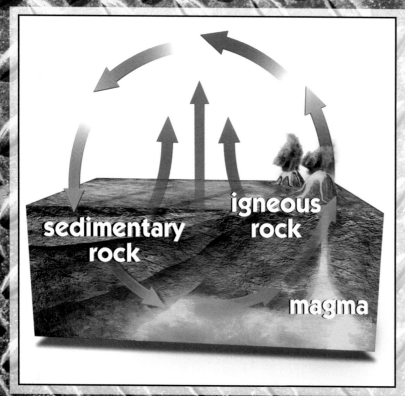

sedimentary rock

igneous rock

magma

The rock cycle

When a volcano erupts, magma spews out as lava. Lava cools and hardens into igneous rock. As weather **erodes** igneous rock over time, it breaks into small pieces called particles. The rock particles settle and pile up in layers. This type of rock is called sedimentary rock. Some sedimentary rock melts into the hot layer of the Earth and becomes magma.

Metallic veins

Magma that rises from within the Earth during a volcanic eruption does not always reach the surface. As magma pushes its way upward it can enter fractures, or cracks, in the Earth's crust, where it becomes trapped and eventually cools and hardens into rock. If the magma contains enough metal minerals, veins of metal ore deposits form in the fractures.

Lode and placer deposits

Metal ore deposits that are **embedded** in solid igneous rock are known as lode deposits. Over time, rain and wind erode small metal particles. The particles wash away and collect in river and stream beds. These types of deposits are called placer deposits.

(above) Miners who pan streams for gold are seeking placer deposits.

(below) Veins of metal deposits form in cracks in the Earth's crust.

veins

mineral rich
magma

Metal ages

The discovery of metal changed the lives of people in the ancient world. Metals made agriculture easier, providing farmers with more efficient tools to work their land. Armies that possessed metal knives, swords, and shields were no match for those that did not. The first two metals widely used by humans, copper and gold, are still important in people's lives today.

Copper Age

Copper came into common use between 6000 B.C. and 4000 B.C. Copper is a red-colored metal that is easy to shape. In ancient times, nuggets of pure copper were found lying on the Earth's surface. Copper's distinctive color made it easy for ancient peoples to locate, and its ductility made the metal useful for many purposes.

Most copper is embedded in ore. Copper was the first metal to be extracted from ore. After people learned how to separate the copper, by a process called **annealing**, they used the metal to make decorations, farming tools, and weapons of war. Ancient civilizations in Mesopotamia, the area that is now Iraq, were among the first to learn how to use copper. The Mediterranean, especially the island of Cyprus, provided an abundant source of copper for the ancient world.

These axes were made during the Bronze Age. They were found in present-day Italy.

Bronze Age

Between 4000 B.C. and 3000 B.C., people began making bronze by combining copper and tin. Bronze was useful because it was stronger and more durable than either copper or tin alone.

The Bronze Age lasted until about 1000 B.C. Early bronze uses included making containers, such as cups, **urns**, and vases, but the metal was also used to make tools and weapons. Bronze was used in Egypt beginning in about 2000 B.C. to make statues. To make statues, the Egyptians used a method called the lost-wax process. A mold was made out of wax in the shape of the statue. Clay was set around the wax. When the clay was fired and hardened, the wax melted and dripped out. The bronze was heated until it could be poured into the clay cast. When the metal hardened, the clay was broken and the bronze statue revealed.

The dagger on the left is made of copper. The one on the right is bronze.

Space-aged iron

Meteorites were a source of metals in the ancient world. Aboriginal cultures in Greenland and Mexico extracted iron and other metals from meteorites that fell from outer space. Three meteorites found in Greenland by American explorer Robert Edwin Peary in 1894 were long used by the Inuit people as a source of metal to make knives and other weapons.

The Ahnighito meteorite is the second largest meteorite on Earth. It landed in Greenland, but was later brought to New York. It was a source of iron for the Inuit peoples.

11

Weapons of war

For almost as long as humans have used metals, they have used them to make weapons of war. In the Copper and Bronze Ages, people used copper and bronze to make weapons including daggers, shields, and swords. The creation of strong iron in the Iron Age improved the quality of weapons. In the Middle Ages, a time period from 500 A.D. to 1500 A.D. in Western Europe, metal was used to make suits of armor worn by knights in battle. The 1300s saw the beginning of improved ironworking techniques, brought on by the invention of firearms. Iron was also essential in **World War II**, when the United States required the metal to construct weapons for its war effort. Iron remains a crucial metal in constructing weapons of war, including tanks, planes, ships, and missiles.

This illustration shows a metalworker shaping a farm tool from iron.

Iron Age

About 1500 B.C., in present-day Turkey, a method of getting iron from ore was developed. To get iron, a very high temperature was needed to melt the metal and remove the **oxygen** from the ore. This was accomplished using **charcoal** fires. Over the next 500 years, the use of iron spread across Europe, Asia, and Africa.

Steel

Until the 1600s, only thin pieces of iron could be made that were suitable for making swords. When **coal** started to be used to heat furnaces, larger quantities of stronger iron were produced. In the 1800s, a stronger metal was made when English inventor Henry Bessemer developed a method for making steel. Steel was stronger than iron and could be used to make skyscrapers, large bridges, and stronger train tracks. Today, we are still living in the Iron Age.

A golden metal

Gold is a lustrous, yellow metal that has long been sought after for its natural shine. Decorative gold artifacts found in the royal tombs in Mesopotamia date back to as early as 3000 B.C. Ancient Egyptians also used gold to decorate the tombs of their pharaohs, or

Gold was used by people in Egypt as early as 3500 B.C. to make jewelry and decorations. This golden vulture was a collar placed around the neck of an Egyptian pharaoh named Tutankhamun after his death.

kings. European explorers came to America in search of gold. The value of gold has inspired many to explore for it over time, including prospectors who gave up all their possessions to search for gold in Alaska in the early 1900s.

Gold became a **currency** used to trade goods and services around 1500 B.C. Until the 1970s, gold was the standard by which the value of international currencies, such as the American dollar, were measured.

13

Locations of metals

Different types of metal ore are mined in countries all around the world. A metal ore deposit is valuable to a country because it creates jobs, can be extracted and sold to other countries, and can be used to make goods. Together, all these things strengthen a country's economy.

Aluminum

Aluminum is a shiny silver-white metal that is easy to shape. The most abundant metal in the Earth's crust, aluminum is mainly found in a type of ore called bauxite. Major **reserves** are located in Guinea, Australia, Brazil, Jamaica, and India.

Copper

Chile, the United States, and Indonesia are the largest producers of copper ore. A highly ductile, red-colored metal, copper is one of the most common metals found in nature.

Gold

South Africa possesses about half of the world's gold resources, but significant deposits of the shiny yellow metal are also found in the United States, Australia, Brazil, Canada, China, and Russia.

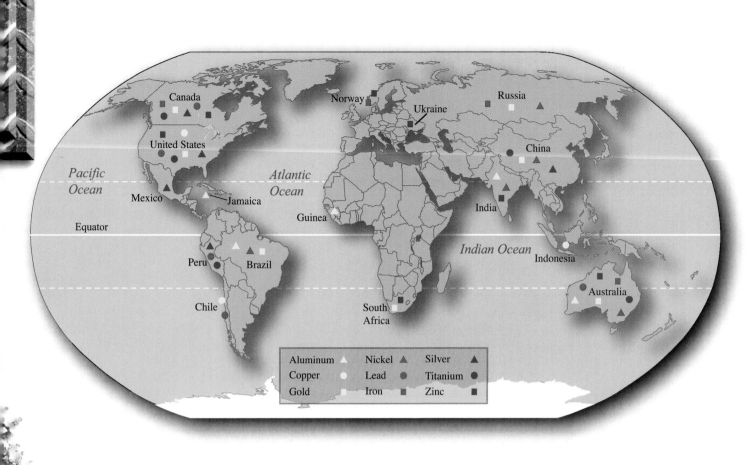

The map shows the countries of the world with major deposits of some of the most commonly used metals.

Iron ore

The world's major producers of iron ore include Australia, Brazil, China, Russia, and India, but iron is found in most parts of the world. About 98 percent of mined iron ore is used to make steel. Steel is an important metal to the world economy. Hematite, limonite, and magnetite are types of ore that contain iron.

Lead

Lead is a heavy, soft blue-white metal used in making many common products, including batteries and televisions. Most of the world's lead is produced by the United States, but Australia, Canada, China, and Peru also possess significant reserves.

Nickel

Nickel is a shiny, hard silver-white metal that is highly resistant to corrosion. Major nickel producers include Australia, Canada, Norway, and Russia, but significant nickel reserves are also found in Cuba, Indonesia, and the Philippines.

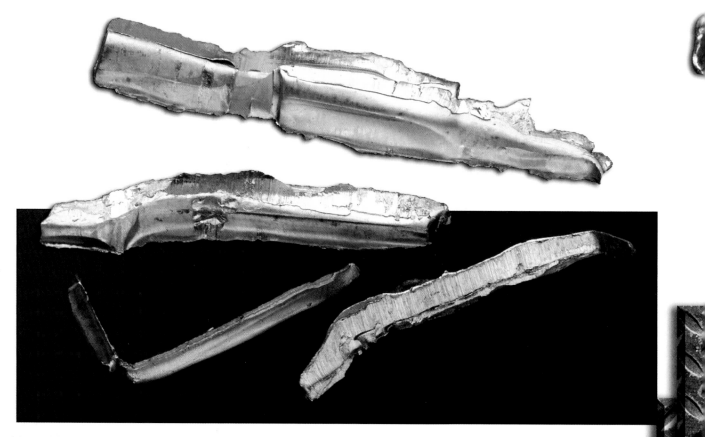

Silver

Silver is a white, lustrous metal found in countries including the United States, Canada, Mexico, Peru, and China. Most silver is used to make coins, jewelry, and utensils. Silver is often alloyed with copper to make it harder.

Zinc

Close to 40 countries around the globe mine zinc, a blue-white colored metal used in making car parts. Major producers include China, Australia, Peru, Canada, and the United States.

Titanium

Titanium is a light, strong silver-gray metal. Deposits are found in Australia, Canada, India, Norway, South Africa, Ukraine, and the United States. Titanium is alloyed with aluminum and iron to be used to make aircraft parts. It is stronger and lighter than steel.

Finding ore deposits

Geologists are scientists who study the Earth. They use both their knowledge and a variety of scientific equipment to locate metal ore deposits. In ancient times, explorers seeking metal ore did not have today's modern technology at their disposal. Instead, they relied on their sight and knowledge of an area's geographical features to guide them. Modern geologists identify metal ore deposits in several different ways.

Observation

Geologists begin to look for ore deposits by conducting a general inspection of an area by air or land vehicle. Geologists examine the structure and shape of rock masses to determine if ore might be present, and look for the visible presence of metal mineral **crystals**. Before conducting a general inspection, geologists often use computers to access reports that provide geological information on an area they believe an ore deposit may be located. **Satellite** and aerial photographs also provide clues to the presence of ore deposits. This information helps geologists identify different types of rock and rock structures in an area. Aircraft equipped with specialized instruments that measure the properties of rock are also used to gather data.

A geologist in a desert in the South American country of Chile uses specialized electronic equipment to test underground rock for conductivity.

Ground survey

If an area looks like it contains an ore deposit, a more detailed ground survey is planned. This means geologists travel to an area thought to contain ore and test the properties of the rock there. The **magnetic** property of rock can reveal the presence of an ore deposit, so geologists send an electrical **current** into a rock mass to determine if ore is present. This is done using an instrument called a magnetometer. X-rays, or rays of **energy** that pass through solid objects, also help geologists identify the presence of metal deposits by revealing the structure of underground rock formations. After gathering enough information about an area under exploration, geologists create a detailed geological map.

Sampling

When a possible ore deposit is identified, geologists use drills to burrow into the surface of the Earth and collect rock samples. Different types of drilling instruments are used to gather the samples depending on how deep into the Earth an ore deposit is thought to be located. Each rock sample collected by a geologist is carefully cataloged. Geologists test the samples in a laboratory using specialized equipment that indicates if the rock contains metals.

(top) A geologist handling rock samples.

(below) The wires in this aircraft measure the magnetic properties of the rock on the ground as the plane flies overhead.

Mining

Once geologists have determined that metal ore exists in an area, the mining, or extraction, process begins. Today's technology allows people to extract metal ore from the Earth much more easily than in ancient times, when miners used shovels and buckets to do the job. Technology has also allowed people to extract and process ore located in hard to reach places, such as deposits buried deep underground.

Extracting the ore

Deposits of metal ore take different forms. Lode deposits, or metal embedded in solid rock, require mining to extract. Metals are generally found in small quantities of ore, which means large amounts of rock must be removed from an area to get the metals they contain. The two main ways to mine lode deposits are underground and open-pit mining.

A drilling machine is used to make holes in which explosives are placed.

Underground mining

Metal ore buried deep under the Earth's surface is dug out by underground mining. Miners who extract ore from underground mines dig and use explosives to create long and narrow passages down into the Earth. These passages are called shafts. Tunnels are dug or blasted using explosives. Miners extract ore from the tunnels, transporting it up the mine shafts and to the surface using elevators. At the surface, the ore is transported by truck or rail to a mill.

Open-pit mining

Open-pit mining, also known as strip mining, is used to extract ore deposits located closer to the Earth's surface. Miners make shallow cuts into the Earth, and then use machines and shovels to extract ore before transporting it to a mill.

While open-pit mining is less expensive than underground mining, it has a high environmental cost, leaving visible scars on the Earth.

A dangerous job

A miner's work involves many hazards. Unexpected rock slides, floods, and explosions have killed many miners through history. Over time, technology has helped make mines safer places for people to be. Before going to work, a modern miner puts on protective clothing, including boots, a hard hat, and safety glasses. Modern miners are well trained to handle their dangerous work. Poor air quality was once a major problem for underground miners, but improved **ventilation systems** have made mines easier places to breathe. Better communications equipment and systems have helped reduce the number of mining accidents involved in using explosives and drilling.

A miner reads the last message written by another miner trapped in a mining accident. The message says, "Three o'clock gas is getting strong."

Milling and smelting

Ore is taken to a mill where it is smelted. The smelting process separates pure metals from the ore that contains them. Different smelting processes are used for different kinds of metals. The earliest metalworkers separated metal from ore using the heat of a fire, which melted the metal and separated it from rock. Over time, people have learned to improve the smelting process, making it easier and more efficient to extract metals from rock.

The crushed ore after leaching at a gold mine is dumped into piles.

Leaching

Leaching is the first step in **refining** metal ore. During the leaching process, workers run machines that crush metal ore into a powder. After this, as much waste rock as possible is removed from the powder. In iron production, this is done by using large magnets that separate metal from rock and other elements. In gold production, powdered ore is mixed in a tank with water and chemicals, a process known as floatation, which separates the gold from rock and other substances.

High heat

After the leaching process, the crushed ore is put in a furnace that reaches temperatures high enough to melt it. Mill employees who operate the furnace work under hot conditions. Depending on the type of metal, different chemicals are added to separate the molten, or melted, metal from other elements that remained in the crushed ore. The unwanted elements are called slag. Slag is removed from the furnace before the molten metal. Workers operate machines that remove molten metal from the furnace and cast, or shape, it into a desired form.

Important industries

Early metal smelting operations generally produced small amounts of metal. Today's mills produce more metals than ever before and provide jobs for thousands of workers in the place where they are located. Milling and smelting operations are important to every industrial economy in the world because they produce metals crucial to manufacturing.

A steel worker at a mill separates slag from metal in a large vat.

Uses of metals

Metals are everywhere. From constructing the buildings that make up cities, to small electronic devices, metals are used for millions of purposes.

Industry

Metals have countless uses in modern industry, and are used in manufacturing most every product. The **aerospace industry** requires strong, lightweight, and corrosion-resistant metals, such as titanium, to construct airplanes. Iron and steel are widely used in manufacturing industries because they are strong and durable. The machines used to manufacture products on every assembly line contain some steel or iron. The metal zinc is also widely used in industry as a protective coating for iron and steel. Metals are also important in agricultural industries, where they are used to make tractors, combines, and planting machines. The medical industry also relies on metals. Gold, silver, and platinum are all used to make medical instruments.

Technology

Copper is used in high-tech industries because it is a good conductor of electricity. Hidden inside computers, copper is used to transfer electrical currents that make computers work. The inside of every electronic device, including toys and video games, contains some metal parts. Precious metals, such as gold, silver, and platinum are also used in making computers and other electronic devices.

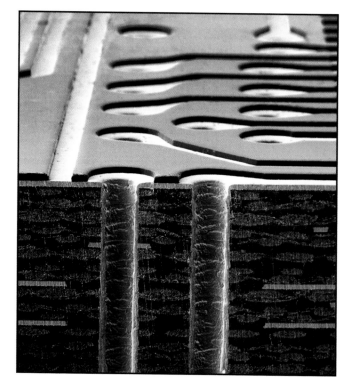

This cross-section of a computer circuit board shows its copper parts.

Construction

Iron and steel are used to construct buildings and bridges because they are strong and durable. Aluminum is used to make window frames and siding on homes because it is lightweight and does not easily rust.

Household metals

Refrigerators, microwaves, and stoves are made with metal, including strong stainless steel. Nickel is one of the metals used to make stainless steel alloys. Tin cans, made of strong steel coated with corrosion-resistant tin, are used to preserve food. A **versatile** metal, aluminum is also used to make aluminum foil.

Transportation

Cars, buses, trucks, trains, and boats are all made with strong metals such as iron and steel. The tracks that trains, streetcars, and subways travel on are also made of iron and steel.

Decoration

The lustrous metals gold, silver, and platinum are popular for decoration. They are used to make rings, necklaces, and earrings. Copper is another metal used for decorative purposes. Copper is used to make statues, including the Statue of Liberty in New York.

Steel

Steel is the most common and important metal used today. Almost every product people use in their daily lives contains some amount of steel. Steel is a popular metal because it is strong, widely available, and can be easily shaped into a desired object. Steel is an alloy, made by combining iron with carbon and small amounts of other elements.

Steel classifications

Steels are classified according to the amount of carbon they contain. The more carbon a steel has, the harder and more durable it is. The least durable steels, known as mild steels, contain up to 0.25 percent carbon. Medium carbon steels contain between 0.25 percent and 0.45 percent carbon. High carbon steel contains up to 1.5 percent carbon.

Rust

Rust is a red-brown coating that forms on iron that is exposed to rain and other elements. Rust occurs when water and oxygen create a chemical reaction called oxidization, which deteriorates iron. The more something made of iron rusts, the weaker it gets. The rusting of steel used for bridges poses serious safety problems. Rusting is prevented by galvanizing steel, which is the process of coating it with zinc, as well as by painting or coating unprotected metal.

How steel is made

The main ingredient needed to make steel is the molten metal produced by refining iron ore. This hot, liquid iron is known as pig iron. Iron is melted in a **blast furnace,** which creates temperatures high enough to keep metal in a liquid form. The first step in making steel is putting scrap iron, or recycled iron, into a blast furnace. Steel can consist of up to 30 percent scrap iron. The more scrap iron that is in steel, the stronger the finished product. After scrap iron is put in the blast furnace, molten pig iron is added. After the molten pig iron and scrap iron are combined, different metals and substances are added, which are different depending on the type of steel being made. There are many types of steel, all with different elements added to achieve a desired strength. When the metal titanium is added during the steel making process, the resulting metal is strong enough to use in making state-of-the-art airplanes and spacecraft. Metals such as nickel and chromium can be added to steel to make many steel alloys, including stainless steel. Silicon is also an important ingredient in making many steel alloys.

Oxygen furnace

1 pig iron from blast furnace

2 oxygen is blown in

3 steel is made

In an oxygen furnace, a fast moving stream of oxygen is added to the pig iron to create a chemical reaction called oxidization that creates steel.

Pollution

Metals make people's lives easier, but the process of extracting them from the Earth has an environmental cost. Not only do ore mining operations leave permanent scars on the landscape, they can also contaminate land and water with harmful chemicals.

Mining

Much of the environmental damage caused by an underground mine is not visible, as ore is extracted from beneath the Earth's surface, usually far from populated areas. Underground mines can collapse, trapping people inside. Modern mines are built more securely, with reinforced roofs and beams. Older, abandoned mines are unsafe for people who carelessly venture into them. Open-pit mines leave enormous craters in the landscape that forever alter the environment. In recent years, many sites where open-pit mines once operated have been reclaimed, meaning soil and plant life have been re-introduced to these areas. The hope is that these sites may one day return to a near-natural state.

People inspecting abandoned equipment in a deserted underground mine.

Refining

Poisonous chemicals used in refining metals, such as the cyanide used in gold production, can kill plant and animal life if they seep into the environment near mining operations. Contaminated waste rock, left over after metal is extracted from ore, is dumped at outdoor storage sites and can also contaminate soil and water. Mining companies are always striving to lessen the impact of mining on the environment, seeking safer ways to store and dispose of waste rock and make mining safer.

The slag, or waste, from metal refining is dumped into the ground, which poisons the soil.

The heavy, silver-colored metal mercury is extremely poisonous and is deadly if released into the environment. Different from all other metals in that it remains liquid at room temperature, mercury is widely used in making electronic devices and medical instruments.

Recycling

The recycling of metals has been going on since humans discovered them. In the Copper Age, tools and weapons were melted down and reformed into new objects. The use of scrap iron in making steel is an example of modern recycling. No matter how many times a metal is melted and reformed, it remains as good as new.

New practices

One of the most familiar symbols of modern metal recycling is the recycling bin, used to discard used metal cans and beverage containers. In some parts of the world, people separate metals from other types of garbage in their homes and place them in a recycling bin, which is collected by workers and taken to a recycling plant. At the recycling plant, metals are melted down to be reused. Reusing metal means there is less garbage going into landfill sites, or dumps, and less metal will need to be mined in the future.

At the recycling plant, metal containers are separated on a long conveyor belt.

A crane is used to collect scrap metal that will be melted down and made into new metal.

The future of metals

The Earth's supply of metals can not last forever. If humans continue to use metals at the current rate of **consumption**, the world's reserves of many metals will one day run out. To prevent metals from being used up, it is important that people continue to recycle and develop alternatives to commonly used metals.

Wartime recycling

During World War II, the demand for metal increased because it was used to make the many bombs, guns, boats, and tanks for soldiers in Europe. After Japan invaded nations where the metal was mined, the **Allies** faced a shortage of metal supply. In need of tin for the war effort, the U.S. began a recycling program that called on citizens to recycle tin cans. Community groups across the nation, including the Boy Scouts, pitched in and gathered thousands of tons of cans.

Posters during World War II encouraged civilians to recycle.

Glossary

abundant Found in a large amount

aerospace industry The science of building aircraft to venture into outer space

Allies The nations that fought together in World War II, including Britain, France, the United States, and the Soviet Union

annealing The process of heating and then cooling to strengthen

atmosphere The layers of gases surrounding the Earth

blast furnace A furnace in which combustion is intensified by a blast of air

carbon A non-metallic element found in all living things

charcoal A fuel made from trees or other plant or animal material containing carbon

coal A fuel formed from the ancient remains of decayed plants

conductor A substance through which heat or electricity can easily pass

consumption Using something up

contaminate To make impure, or unclean

corrosion The process of gradually wearing away

crystals Solid pieces of a substance that have regular arrangements of flat surfaces and angles

currency Money

current A flow of electricity

deteriorate To weaken or rot over time

economy The way a country organizes and manages its businesses, industries, and money

electricity A form of energy that occurs naturally or is artificially produced and used to create light and heat

elements A group of 100 substances that each has its own kind of atoms

embedded Firmly fixed in a surrounding substance

energy Power for doing work

erodes Being worn away, usually by water or wind

magnetic Able to attract iron and steel

meteorite A giant ball of rock and metal that travels through space and lands on earth

oxygen The gas we breathe

pressure The force, or weight, that presses on an object

refining Removing unwanted material from a substance

reserve A supply of something to be used at a later date

resistant Able to withstand an effect

satellite A body in space that orbits Earth

urn A large vase

ventilation systems Machines used to make the air cleaner

versatile Able to do many things well

World War II A war fought from 1939 to 1945 in which Great Britain, France, the Soviet Union, the U.S., and other Allies defeated Germany, Italy, and Japan

Index